Lies, Damned Lies and Statistics

LIES Damned LIES AND STATISTICS

How Obsolete Stats, Hidebound Thinking, and
Human Bias Create College Football Controversies

MIKE NEMETH

NEW YORK

LONDON • NASHVILLE • MELBOURNE • VANCOUVER

Lies, Damned Lies and Statistics

How Obsolete Stats, Hidebound Thinking, and Human Bias Create College Football Controversies

Published in New York, New York, by Morgan James Publishing. Morgan James is a trademark of Morgan James, LLC. www.MorganJamesPublishing.com

The Morgan James Speakers Group can bring authors to your live event. For more information or to book an event visit The Morgan James Speakers Group at www.TheMorganJamesSpeakersGroup.com.

ISBN 9781683508571 paperback
ISBN 9781683508588 eBook
Library of Congress Control Number: 2017960710

Cover and Interior Design by:
Chris Treccani www.3dogcreative.net

In an effort to support local communities, raise awareness and funds, Morgan James Publishing donates a percentage of all book sales for the life of each book to Habitat for Humanity Peninsula and Greater Williamsburg.

Get involved today! Visit www.MorganJamesBuilds.com

For Angie
My love and inspiration.

There are lies, damned lies and statistics.

—Mark Twain

TABLE OF CONTENTS

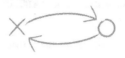

CHAPTER ONE

Blame It on *Moneyball*

All truth passes through three stages.
First, it is ridiculed.
Second, it is violently opposed.
Third, it is accepted as being self-evident.
—Arthur Schopenhauer

Like new immigrants learning a foreign language, young fans first learn the fundamentals of college football by watching television. Televised broadcasts of the games teach us what we pretend to know about the game before we try out for our first Pop Warner team. The play-by-play announcers and their color commentating "expert" sidekicks deliver the lessons like grammar school teachers explaining the difference between whole numbers and fractions. The most authoritative voices are those of the coaches. Conventional football wisdom—coach speak—can be summed up in just a few sentences that every fan hears hundreds of times during any football season:

1. Turnovers win football games.
2. Run the ball and stop the run to win football games.
3. Control the ball to control the clock to win football games.
4. Convert third downs on offense and stop third down conversions on defense to win football games.

As we mature, we accept this boring prescription for football excellence and tune out when sideline reporters ask their redundant questions and receive their redundant answers.

Then I read *Moneyball* by Michael Lewis (*The Blind Side*, *The Big Short*), and it raised the possibility that football doesn't work the way we've been taught to think it works. The basic premise of his book: Baseball "experts," coaches, managers, front office executives, players, and the media had collected an exhaustive array of statistics about the game for more than 100 years, and yet they had overlooked the statistics that were key to success at the game.

Despite working with a shoestring budget, the Oakland A's became a competitive franchise by exploiting analytics, the dark science mistrusted by the sports community. Baseball "experts" doubted the analytics would produce wins because the A's didn't pass the exalted "eyeball test." While opposing players flew around the bases after hits, the A's players more often moved station to station after walks.

But the wins piled up, and the A's paid less per victory than their opponents. Soon other franchises employed nerds to parse the numbers and find secrets and advantages overlooked by hidebound experts for decades.

Baseball is not an Outlier

If it could happen in baseball, couldn't it happen in basketball, a game adorned with relatively few statistics? I researched the correlation between traditional basketball statistics and winning basketball games and found that the traditional stats did not have a cause-and-effect relationship with winning. Teams could dominate their opponents in the traditional statistical categories and still lose; teams could be dominated in the traditional statistical categories and yet win. I called these odd games "Black Swans" because they proved that not all games could be explained by traditional statistics (not all swans are white).

That meant that evaluations of basketball teams, based upon the misleading statistics, were misguided. And that invitations to the national championship tournament and seedings in the field were often wrong. And, finally, that undeserving champions sometimes walked away with the trophy.

So I invented a new set of basketball metrics that consistently explain game results and accurately value teams for the quality of their play. I published the results in a book called *128 Billion to 1* (the odds against picking a perfect March Madness™ bracket).

If it could happen in baseball *and* basketball, couldn't it happen in football as well? What if the four platitudes at the start of this chapter—coach speak—have no relationship to winning football games? What if coaches are "dumbing it down" for the fans when they exchange their tired homilies with sideline reporters? What if traditional football statistics have little correlation with winning? What if, like baseball and basketball, college football has suffered for more than a century for lack of good statistics to explain the mechanics of the game?

More importantly, what if the College Football Playoff (CFP) committee members (the CFP committee consists of thirteen men who select the four teams to play for the national championship) are misinformed and misguided by faulty statistics? What if they've chosen the wrong teams? What if incorrect seedings have prescribed the wrong matchups? What if the wrong teams have walked away with the championship trophy?

As the quote from Schopenhauer predicts, if my suspicion that football fans and experts have been systematically misinformed is true, the truth will be ridiculed and opposed before it is accepted as self-evident. So let's get the process started.

CHAPTER TWO

Circumstantial Evidence

*Believe only half of what you see and
nothing that you hear.*
—Edgar Allan Poe

The College Football Playoff rankings are a welcome diversion as the weather transitions from the stifling heat of summer to the punishing cold of winter. They also change the course of history. The four teams chosen to compete in the playoff receive financial advantages, recruiting advantages, and reputational brand advantages, that improve their performance for years after their appearance in the playoff. The record books indelibly reflect the achievement of the chosen few. And, every child's memories of the playoff last a lifetime.

The CFP committee ranks twenty-five teams (out of a population of 130 teams in the Football Bowl Subdivision (FBS), formerly known as Division I) based upon an "… evaluation of the teams' performance on the field." No explanation is provided as to how the evaluation occurs, but four factors receive the most press attention as the season progresses:

1. Won and lost records;
2. Strength of Schedule;
3. Statistics and analytics; and,
4. The eyeball test.

Tie-breaking factors listed on the committee Website include:

1. Conference championships;
2. Head-to-head results; and,
3. Results against common opponents.

At first glance, these criteria seem reasonable, even thoughtful. Under closer scrutiny, these criteria fail to produce controversy-free rankings.

Distorted Inputs

The most natural way to evaluate teams is to watch the games and form subjective opinions. The media calls this the "eyeball test." Experts believe they can judge whether one or both teams played well simply by watching them play. Reliance on the eyeball test leaves me as queasy as I would be if my physician told me that since I look healthy I needn't worry about my blackouts or the numbness in my left arm.

Typically, too much credit is assigned to margin of victory. Typically, too much credit goes to offense and not enough to defense. And, too often, our eyeballs are pleased by a team that plays at a fast pace and not enough by a team that plays slower. Games played at a fast pace with a high offensive output are more fun to watch and thus we think more highly of the winner of such games. During 2017, Oklahoma received a lot of questionable credit for being fun to watch.

The heralded eyeball test fails in another critical dimension: It is virtually impossible for any viewer, whether fan or expert, to adjust his evaluation of team performance based upon the strength of the opponent. A good performance leaves an indelible impression on the brain whether the opponent was strong or weak. The reverse is true as well.

The 2017 CFP committee included five former head football coaches. Coaches watch tape to evaluate teams. When they watch tape, coaches look for effective schemes, assignment discipline, player talent, and team effort, all nearly impossible to quantify and compare. To be useful in a ranking mechanism, these factors would have to be quantified relative to the results they produced. It isn't enough to play the game the way coaches want their teams to play.

The undeniable conclusion: While watching games is entertainment, it is not suitable input for comparative evaluation. This precept is just as true for the selection committee expert as it is for the fan in his living room—though the expert's ego may lead him to reject the truth.

Best Teams or Best Records?

There are no published, hard-and-fast rules that the committee members are compelled to follow. There is no transparency surrounding their judgments as their votes are not made public.

We know after four years of interpreting committee rankings that won/lost records are the primary inputs to their evaluation process because won/lost records are used to explain their rankings. The committee establishes a pecking order, based upon won/lost records, in its first release of rankings and then demotes losers and backfills with winners in each subsequent weekly ranking. Rarely does the committee demote a winner, or promote a loser, based upon how well it played or how good its opponent was. That wouldn't seem logical to fans who've been conditioned to respect won/lost records above all other factors. In fact, everyone who has grown up inside the game shares the same misguided devotion to the won/lost record. People who've played the game have been conditioned to view their won/lost record as the ultimate evidence of their worth as athletes.

As the CFP committee selects teams for the playoff, the temptation to favor teams with better won/lost records, head-to-head victories, more wins perceived to be "good", or fewer losses perceived to be "bad", is irresistible.

You Are What Your Record Says You Are

A famous professional football coach has said it's so. Of course, he's talking about an organized league where schedules, the draft, and payroll rules are designed to level the playing field. Such is not the case in college football. Some schools have, and exploit, greater resources than others. Schedules are unequal. Recruiting classes and talent levels vary widely. Nonetheless, the CFP committee members intuit cosmic meaning from wins and losses.

America's obsession with winning ranks near the top of a list that includes sex, celebrities, scandals, cars, and money. In the public perception, winning is good and losing is bad, and there isn't anything very complicated about the matter. Winning is the only objective of the games we play, so it seems logical to gauge the quality of a team by the number in its win column.

As unassailable as this logic seems to be, it is the "logic" that sparks the controversy surrounding the playoff and fuels debate over the rankings. This faulty logic causes the arguments between you and your neighbor over the backyard fence.

"Win" and "lose" are like pass or fail grades on a test in school; they are binary summaries of complex events, and much information is lost in the summation. Take, for example, a situation in which four students score 99, 71, 69, and 29 on the same math test. If the test is graded on a pass/fail basis with a score of 70 being the minimum requirement to pass, two students fail the test and two students pass. As a result, the passing scores of 99 and 71 become equivalent and the failing scores of 69 and 29 become equivalent, but the gulf between the 71 and the 69 is as wide as the Grand Canyon.

Clearly these four students exhibit widely divergent degrees of mathematical competence (a quantitative measure), but that is not apparent with two "passes" and two "fails" (binary measures). "W" and "L" expose the same amount of information as "pass" and "fail," and they also conceal the same amount of information. If we want to know how well these four students know math, we wouldn't limit our investigation to whether they passed or failed the test. We would examine the actual test scores to obtain an accurate assessment. The same is true when comparing wins and losses for football teams.

Now imagine that each of these students took a slightly different test on the same day. That is what college football teams do every Saturday. We wouldn't consider all passing grades to be equally valuable in ranking the students. We would immediately want to know the relative difficulty of each test and the precise numerical score earned by each student. Then we could compare results and make a judgment as to which students were more knowledgeable.

Imagine another scenario in which there are two slightly different tests of equal difficulty. Each test is taken by two students and the rule is that the student with the higher grade on each test is credited with a "pass" and the student with the lower grade on each test is punished with a "fail". This circumstance happens to college football teams every Saturday in the fall. On the first test the students receive grades of 90 and 80, and the 90 grade is given a pass while the 80 grade is given a fail. On the second test, less knowledgeable students score 75 and 55. The student with the grade of 75 gets a pass and the student with the grade of 55 gets a fail. Reasonable people would not argue that the student with a grade of 75 was better than the student with the 80 simply because that student had won an arbitrary contest with a student who only managed a grade of 55. Yet, that's exactly what football experts argue when they value the won/lost record over a scientific assessment (grading) of teams' playing performances (numerical test grades).

The undisputable fact is that a team can play poorly and still win a football game (pass a test) if it plays marginally better than an opponent that plays worse. We've all witnessed games in which a team won "ugly," games in which neither team could "get anything going." As binary statistics, won/lost records treat all wins equally, thus the team that wins "ugly" receives no less credit than the team that dazzles us with its scintillating performance. On its won/lost record, Oklahoma received no less credit for squeaking past weak Baylor and average Kansas State than it did for shocking highly regarded

Ohio State or outgunning ranked TCU and Oklahoma State teams.

Conversely, a team can play well and yet lose if its opponent plays marginally better. In its won/lost record, Ohio State received no more credit for its play in a loss to an elite Oklahoma team than it did when it was demolished by unranked Iowa. The embarrassing outcome added just one "L" to the loss column for the Buckeyes and the committee was left to make a subjective judgment about the two games.

Unlike school tests, college football has no regulated dividing line between a winning grade and a losing grade. There is no established threshold to cross to earn a win. A team merely has to outplay its opponent. That means that winning teams in the rankings can play worse than losing teams in the rankings but receive more credit simply because they outplayed a specific opponent of unknown difficulty.

Rather than illuminate and enlighten, won/lost records obfuscate, conceal information, and deceive fans and experts alike. Records obscure qualitative measures in the same way that pass/fail grades concealed the difference between the passing 75 grade and the failing 80 grade in the example above.

Winning doesn't automatically mean that a team is "good"; it simply means the winning team played *relatively* better than the losing team, on game day, under a certain set of circumstances. Therefore, winning and losing are relative results and not definitive or decisive results. If the circumstances were changed or the teams played a second time, the outcome could well be different.

Won/lost records are merely the sum of pass/fail results for some number of tests without any qualifying information about the difficulty of the tests or the grades achieved on the tests. A student isn't well educated simply because she passes tests; a student passes the tests because she is well educated. The same can be said of college football teams: *A team isn't good because it wins. A team wins because it is good.*

In the analytics world, winning and losing are always outputs, but never inputs. Wins occur when a team earns a better grade than its opponent in a specific game. But, a winning grade must be compared against all other winning—and losing—grades to see where a team ranks relative to its competitors.

If the committee's job is to select the four best teams for the playoff—the teams that are best at playing the game, not the teams with the shiniest records—then it needs a method to judge playing performance while ignoring won/lost records.

CHAPTER THREE

Black Swans

A beautiful theory, killed by a nasty,
ugly little fact.
—Thomas Henry Huxley

CFP committee members are rumored to access various statistics and analytics to support their team evaluations. If they are using any of the traditional statistics that the average fan digests, they are being misled.

Over an eight-year period I collected statistics from 2,166 games played by 172 teams ranked in the top 25. In the years for which I collected traditional statistics—first downs, yards gained, time of possession, penalty yardage and turnovers—these sample teams often won despite trailing in these statistical categories. They should have lost these games, but they didn't. On the flip side of the coin, the sample teams often lost despite rolling up better numbers than their victorious opponents. Traditional statistics imply that they should have won those games, but they didn't. Time-honored traditional statistics do not guarantee a victory and in fact can be overcome even when lesser teams play highly ranked teams. Therefore, traditional statistics do not have a cause-and-effect relationship with winning. In the analytics world we say that traditional statistics are not "deterministic metrics", i.e. they don't represent the factors that determine which team wins and which loses a football game.

An old adage says you can't prove every swan is white, but with a single black swan you prove they are not. The games won despite trailing in traditional statistical categories— or lost despite leading in those statistical categories—are black swans. They are the exceptions that disprove the rule. In this case, the rule—traditional statistics have a cause-and effect relationship with winning and losing— leads to the incorrect assumption that teams with impressive traditional statistics should be revered and highly ranked. This vicious cycle leads to inaccurate rankings, which lead to wrong selections for the College Football Playoff, which lead to undeserving champions.

When I explained black swans to my neighbor, a former NFL star and current college coach, he reacted as though I had told him that Newton got it wrong when he said gravity kept us from flying off the earth into space[1]. He complained that he had been taught from the

---

1   This is not a farfetched theory. See *But What If We're Wrong* by Chuck Klosterman.

age of six to grind out first downs and pile up yardage to win football games, and that's what he teaches his current players. Thus, the self-fulfilling prophecy is perpetuated.

For three seasons, covering 829 games, I collected traditional statistics. After three seasons I stopped wasting time on all but turnovers, the biggest bogeyman of them all.

The table below depicts the relationship of traditional statistics to winning.

STATISTIC	% OF GAMES LED	WON LEADING	LOST LEADING	WON TRAILING
Time of Poss	56.6	87.4	38.3	73.6
First Downs	67.6	88.6	41.6	66.5
Turnovers*	49.5	92.7	16.8	64.5
Total Yards	73.8	91.3	34.4	53.5
Penalties**	45.6	82.0	44.2	80.9

*The turnover statistic covers all eight seasons of statistics collection.

**The penalties statistic is fewer penalty yards, which would be considered the better result.

This table exposes the following truths:

1. Highly ranked teams won games far more often than they led in the traditional statistical categories. During the three seasons in which traditional statistics were collected, sample teams won 81.6 percent of the games they played. This implies that highly ranked teams have qualities and exploit factors that are not represented by traditional statistics.

2. Sample teams won often when trailing in the traditional statistical categories. This implies that we are missing some categories that determined the winning results.

3. Except for turnovers, sample teams lost more often when leading in these categories than they did overall—18.4 percent. My apologies to my NFL retiree/college coach neighbor but this fact proves that the factors represented by traditional statistics are not particularly important.

The Biggest Bogeyman of All

The oft-extoled turnover category appears at first glance to have meaning. Sample teams lost less often than their overall loss percentage while having an advantage in turnovers—16.8 percent as compared to 18.4 percent overall—which implies a weak connection to winning. However, highly ranked teams enjoy a turnover advantage in less than half of their games. Teams win 92.7 percent of the games in which they have a turnover advantage, and they enjoy a turnover advantage in only 49.5 percent of their games. Therefore, they win, and have a turnover advantage at the same time, in 45.9 percent of their games. So it can be said that a turnover advantage may have played some role in nearly half their wins. As was the case for the other statistical categories, highly ranked teams win often (64.5 percent) when they don't have a turnover advantage, which implies that turnover disadvantages can be overcome by factors not measured by traditional statistics.

Coaches fear that turnovers will lead to opponent scores, but this fear is unwarranted. Touchdowns by opponents' defenses and special teams combined for just 6.1 percent of all opponent scoring during the 2017 season, or about 1.2 points per game. More than half of these points are surrendered on kickoff and punt returns and not on pick sixes or scoop-and-score fumble recoveries.

Turnovers in a team's own territory do lead to short field possessions for opponents, and coaches fear that short field possessions are a serious threat to winning football games. The numbers don't justify this fear either. During the 2017 season, only 32.2 percent of sample team giveaways resulted in a short field possession for the opponent. Sample team opponents scored 15.7 percent of their points on short field possessions, or about 3.1 points per game. However, most short field possessions—54.9 percent—were the result of special teams play—kickoff and punt returns, fumbles, onside kicks, blocked kicks, failed fourth down conversions, etc. Assuming an even distribution of scoring across the various causes of a short field possession, sample team opponents scored about 1.4 points per game on short field possessions that resulted from turnovers.

In total, sample team turnovers accounted for about 2 points per game for their opponents. Coaches are hiding under the bedcovers when there is no monster under their beds. There may be a monster in their closets, but it isn't turnovers. Perhaps coaches should worry more about special teams than they do about turnovers.

Sample teams score more points on short field possessions, about 7 points per game, but the difference isn't due to turnovers. Sample teams produce short field possessions from turnovers at essentially the same rate as their opponents: 36.9 percent of sample team takeaways resulted in short field possessions. The difference in scoring is due to the difference in the skill levels between highly ranked teams and unranked teams. Highly ranked teams scored on 73.4 percent of their short field possessions and averaged 4.4 points per short field possession. Highly ranked teams limited their opponents to scoring on 61.9 percent of their short field possessions and to an average of 3.3 points per short field possession.

Most turnovers simply bring a ball possession to a conclusion in the same way as a punt, a failed fourth down attempt, running out of time at the end of a half or end of a game, or, of course, scoring[2]. The effect of turnovers on winning and losing is a myth.

Traditional Statistics Demystified

Teams win games because they outscore their opponents. It follows that traditional statistics don't relate to winning and losing because they don't correlate with scoring. Traditional statistics track team effort, not team results. Under the rules in effect today, all touchdowns count six points whether they were the result of an eighty-yard drive, a twenty-yard drive, or a non-offensive score.

---

2   Turnovers have a negligible influence on game outcomes even though I count safeties, blocked punts and blocked field goals as turnovers ("giveaways").

If we wanted traditional statistics to correlate with scoring (and, thus, with winning), we would have to change how the game is scored. To correlate with yards gained, we would have to award more points for a touchdown drive of eighty yards than for a drive of twenty yards— maybe a scale of one point for every ten yards gained on a successful drive. In other words, we'd reward team effort. To keep yards gained in line with scoring we'd have to subtract yards gained on unsuccessful drives. We would also have to scale field goal points according to the length of the drive that preceded the kick and subtract yards on drives that ended in a missed field goal. We'd also reduce the number of points awarded for non-offensive scores (scores on special teams and defense) so that those points wouldn't skew the relationship between yards gained and offensive points scored. If we wanted turnovers to correlate with winning, we would only count the turnovers that resulted in an opponent score. Taking this logic to its ridiculous conclusion, we'd award first downs for every ten yards gained, add points for time of possession, and add and subtract points for penalties. Then traditional statistics would correlate with scoring and they'd have a cause-and-effect relationship with winning. The more effort a team made, the more points it would score.

Of course, these rule changes would create a very different game in which bad field position potentially would be worth more than good field position, an easy, short field goal kick would be worth more than a longer kick, and game strategies would be turned on their heads. Since traditional statistics are not deterministic statistics given the way scores are counted today, traditional statistics cannot be used to measure how good any one team is nor how good any opponent is.

Seasonal Statistics Debunked

I cringe when I hear TV analysts remark that a certain team leads the nation in total offense or total defense. Seasonal statistics are accumulations of game effort/traditional statistics. As such, they are invalid for qualitative assessments. Seasonal statistics are also "raw" statistics, meaning they are unadjusted for strength of schedule. It makes no sense to compare seasonal statistics for a Power Five conference team to those of a Group of Five conference team.

One must assume that coaches know all these things and give fans watered-down, politically correct, but useless summaries of what happened in a football game in order to make the game more understandable. For more than 100 years, no one has invented team performance statistics that determine and explain the outcome of football games, so I decided to do it.

CHAPTER FOUR

Where is D. B. Cooper?

*Ignorance is preferable to error, and he is less
remote from the truth who believes nothing
than he who believes what is wrong.*
—Thomas Jefferson

For eight years I've expected game announcers
and color analysts to stop talking about yards
gained, first downs, and turnovers, but they
still try to explain games using those unreliable
statistics. For eight years I've waited for the
purveyors of advanced analytics to produce a
new set of statistics that determine and explain

game outcomes, but I'm not aware of any who have. In 1971, Dan Cooper—misidentified by the press as D. B. Cooper—jumped out of a Boeing 727 with a ransom of $200,000 and has never been apprehended. Perhaps he also stole college football's meaningful statistics.

We can trust that the winning team in any game deserves our respect because it has played better in some way than the losing team. Although I hear TV analysts and football experts say that a team outplayed its opponent and yet lost the game, it cannot be true. A team cannot be outplayed and yet win the game, either. The experts are simply looking at the wrong statistics. And, the experts' eyeballs have deceived them. The game would be a meaningless exercise if this weren't true.

This raises the interesting question of whether a team is "good" simply because its opponents are "bad," or is bad simply because its opponents are good. Winning only means that one team played *relatively* better than the other team on game day. Losing only means that one team played *relatively* less well than the other team. Winning and losing are not unusual occurrences. In every contest, one team plays *relatively* better than the other.

Immediately, we are faced with two problems: 1) we don't know how "good" the winning team's opponent happened to be, and 2) we don't have a precise measurement of how well either team played in this game. We'll address playing performance here and strength of opponents in Chapter Seven.

To find a precise measurement of playing performance, we will ignore the traditional statistics that measure effort. As any good businessperson knows, it is a mistake to reward effort when results are the keys to success. As any good statistical analyst knows, statistics that measure effort are useless in the absence of statistics that determine results.

Results are produced in football games when one team outscores the other team. Deterministic statistics, therefore, must correlate with scoring.

The Missing Ingredient

Fans, TV experts, and selection committee members do not have an objective measure of how well a team plays the game. This is the missing ingredient. This measure would be like a student's numerical grade on a specific test. The grade would reveal how well the team played and, over the course of a season, just how good it is, without respect to its won/lost record. Unlike a pass/fail math test, a team would earn a "W" (a pass) if its grade on a test was better than its opponent's grade, and the team would get an "L" (a fail) if its opponent's grade was higher. If the correct, deterministic metrics are used to calculate grades, the winning team will always receive a better grade than the losing team. In other words, this approach will not produce black swans.

One implication of this approach will make hardline traditionalists uncomfortable: It will be possible for one team to earn a better grade in a loss than is earned by another team in a win, just as the student in the last chapter with an 80 was more knowledgeable than the student with a 75 grade. The grading system does not produce or even consider wins and losses (passes and fails). Wins and losses are the result of comparing the grades of the two teams that competed in a single game. In any game, both teams receive an objective grade and the winning team receives the higher grade, but teams that win "ugly" will get lower grades than teams that lose "pretty." The sum of the grades for a season will reveal precisely how good a team is without respect to its won/lost record.

To make the arguments that follow more digestible, I've used a sample of 261 games played by 21 teams from the 2017 football season. These teams include the top 19 teams from the committee's final ranking plus Michigan and Iowa State both of which were in and out of the top 25 during the season. Arguably, these were the best teams of the season.

CHAPTER FIVE

The Definition of Good

*We are drowning in information but
starved for knowledge.*
—John Naisbitt

The definition of a "good" team begins with one simple concept: *Good teams play well.* To measure playing performance, we will have to invent new statistics that determine the outcome of games. The better a team performs in these categories, the more victories it will produce. Even in losses, these new statistics will measure playing performance and assign the correct credit for the loser's performance.

Deterministic Factors

Instead of using wins and losses as an invalid measurement of team performance, we are looking for the reasons *why* teams win, the factors that determine the outcome of football games. So the first question is: How do teams win? And the obvious answer is: They score more points than their opponent. The follow-on question is also obvious: How do teams score (or prevent) points? The table below depicts the division of scoring by our sample teams and their opponents during the 2017 season:

STATISTIC	NON-OFFENSIVE	SHORT FIELD	LONG FIELD
Sample Teams	5.5%	19.9%	74.6%
Points/Game	1.96	7.0	26.4
Opponents	6.1%	15.7%	78.2%
Points/Game	1.18	3.05	15.2

We can draw the following conclusions:

1. Although every head coach can remember a punt return that decided a game, non-offensive points are not material to winning football games.

2. Although every head coach can remember games in which his team turned the ball over in its own territory and surrendered game-winning field goals, opponent short field scoring is rarely decisive.

3. Both highly ranked teams and their opponents score **most of** their points on drives that begin in their own territory (long field drives). An ability to sustain long field drives is the key to winning college football games. Remembering that teams play both sides of the ball, the corollary is: An ability to stop opponent long field

drives is the key to winning college football games. Opponents are somewhat more dependent on long field scoring because their special teams produce fewer scores and fewer short field opportunities.

So how do teams sustain long field drives? I can hear my neighbor saying, "They grind out the yards and rack up the first downs." Sorry, my friend, that is not how long field drives are sustained. First we'll look at why long field drives fail. The chart below breaks down long field possessions for the highly ranked sample teams in 2017.

SCORES	3 & OUT	OFFENSIVE MISTAKES	DEFENSIVE STOPS
39.8%	21.7%	19.3%	19.2%

1. One in five ball possessions failed to launch, but once an initial first down

was converted, sample teams had a 50/50 chance of scoring. That argues for all-out aggression on the first series of plays, but all too often coaches become conservative in their own territory and call two runs into the middle of the line followed by a desperate third down pass. When a first down pass fails, an amazing number of coaches call the run into the middle of the line on second down. On defense, this statistic argues for all-out aggression on an opponent's first series of downs. However, most coaches wait until the opponent has advanced into his territory to begin blitzing and applying pressure on the quarterback.

2. After an initial first down, the sample teams stopped themselves (Offensive Mistakes) on one in four drives by turning the ball over, allowing a sack

or committing a major penalty. This fact would argue for the "bend-but-don't-break" defensive philosophy. If left to their own devices, college offenses will often stop themselves. Offensive mistakes are a major reason why college teams cannot "grind out yards and rack up first downs" to sustain long field drives.

3. On less than one possession out of five, or less than one time in four after an initial first down, sample teams failed to "rack up first downs" but weren't stopped by an offensive mistake. I graciously label these occasions "Defensive Stops," but they are more often caused by a lack of offensive imagination. Offenses that face repeated third down situations are "stopped" by the defense when they fail to convert on third down. Highly ranked offenses faced third down

on 43.7 percent of their series and converted less than half of the third down opportunities (45.15 percent).

Here's a breakdown of long field possessions by sample team opponents (who are usually inferior teams).

SCORES	3 & OUT	OFFENSIVE MISTAKES	DEFENSIVE STOPS
22.4%	31.9%	22.8%	22.9%

Look familiar? Sample team defenses produced more "3 & outs"—or opponent offenses failed more often to achieve an initial first down—but once launched, opponent long field drives resulted in a score once in every three tries. Opponent offenses made more mistakes than did highly ranked offenses, but highly ranked defenses only stopped inferior offenses 3.7 percent more often than inferior defenses stopped highly ranked offenses.

Opponent offenses faced third down on 53.3 percent of their series and converted 35.9 percent. In this case, defensive coordinators can take some credit for forcing more third downs and stopping a high percentage of conversions.

Some initial conclusions can be drawn:

1. Good teams make an initial first down on ball possessions and good teams stop initial first downs by their opponents. Former ESPN analyst Ron Jaworski calls first down "the ignition down." I call the initial first down of a drive the Daddy-can-I-have-the-keys-to-the-family-car down because without the keys that car will not crank and that kid will not pick up his date.

2. Good offenses don't allow sacks and don't commit major violations. Good defenses focus on quarterback pressure

to induce holding penalties, to sack the quarterback or cause a turnover.

3. Most importantly, good offenses execute well on first and second down and *avoid* third down situations. A good third down conversion percentage (anything over 50 percent) isn't necessarily a badge of honor. It could mean that the offense is failing too often on first and second down.

Even my dog is now wondering if I'll ever get around to explaining the successful long field possessions, the ones that result in a score. Spoiler alert: Explosive plays that cover 25 or more yards fuel the long field possessions that result in a field goal or touchdown. In the absence of an explosive play, a defensive major penalty is somewhat helpful. Here are the statistics:

	SCORING DRIVES W/ EXPLOSIVE PLAY	SUCCESS RATE	SCORING DRIVES W/ DEFENSIVE MAJOR PENALTY	SCORING DRIVES W/O SUSTAINING ELEMENT	SUCCESS RATE
Sample Teams	61.2%	85.2%	10.01%	28.83%	17.03%
Opponents	58.43%	73.22%	12.02%	29.45%	8.32%

Color commentators and analysts talk about explosive plays as though they were as rare and awesome as comet sightings. In fact, both highly ranked teams and their opponents produced explosive plays with regularity. Color commentators and analysts typically label plays covering 20 or more yards "explosive," but my research revealed that, unlike the arbitrary measure of 20 yards, a 25-yard standard achieves a deterministic frequency and success rate.

What we learn from these statistics:

1. The majority of sample team scoring drives—**71.2 percent**—are "sustained" because the offense produces an

explosive play or the opponent's defense provides the gift of a major penalty. These drives produce 18.8 points per game.

2. Most opponent scoring drives—70.45 percent—are "sustained" because the offense produces an explosive play, or the highly ranked defense provides the gift of a major penalty. These drives produce 10.7 points per game.

3. Without an explosive play or defensive major penalty, highly ranked teams would score just 7.6 points per game on long field possessions. Without an explosive play or defensive major penalty, sample team opponents would score just 4.5 points per game on long field possessions. Without explosive plays, the average score of a college football game would be: highly ranked teams – 16.5, opponents – 8.7.

4. Explosive plays rarely fail to produce points. Highly ranked teams scored on 85.2 percent of the possessions in which they produced an explosive play. Inferior offenses playing against superior defenses scored on 73.22 percent of the long field possessions in which they produced an explosive play. Obviously, offenses should adopt the Earl Weaver approach and swing for the fences while defenses should play prevent football.

College football teams do not grind out the yards and rack up the first downs to sustain long field scoring drives. Even the teams that are best at execution and overstocked with talent rely upon explosive plays to score points. The two best offenses in 2017 belonged to Oklahoma and Central Florida. Fifty-three of Oklahoma's 77 long field scoring drives—68.8 percent—

and 45 of Central Florida's 67 long field scoring drives—67.2 percent—were produced with the help of an explosive play. If a team wants to score in college football, it must hit home runs.

Note that we've made no mention of whether teams advance the ball by running or by passing, nor whether the explosive plays are passes or scrambles or designed runs. Statistically, it does not matter whether a team is run-oriented or pass-oriented. It matters only that a team can launch a drive with an initial first down and convert an explosive play somewhere along the line. Running versus passing is a question of coaching philosophy, playing style, roster composition, and opponent weaknesses. If a team is good, it will leverage its own capabilities and exploit its opponents' weaknesses to convert an initial first down and add an explosive play.

The Grass Is Always Greener …

… on the other side of the 50 yard line. Imagine a ruler with yards decreasing from 100 to zero on one edge and the probability of scoring increasing from near zero to near 100 percent on the other edge. Field position works like that ruler. The more grass that lies between an initial line of scrimmage and the end zone, the less likely the team is to score. When our sample teams took possession of the ball in their own territory, they had a 39.8 percent chance to score. However, if sample teams took possession in enemy territory, their chances to score soared to 73.4 percent.

Field position is the final factor that affects long field scoring. Special team plays—punts, punt returns, and kickoff returns—most often determine the field position for a fresh ball possession and become secondary factors influencing long field scoring.

This season, sample teams attempted to return 560 kickoffs and lost yardage as compared with a touchback on 294 returns (a 52.5 percent failure rate). The numbers say that a team will gain better field position by not returning kickoffs that can be downed for a touchback. Sample teams' opponents attempted 880 returns and failed to reach the 25 yard line 539 times (a 61 percent failure rate). That means kickoffs should be left short of the goal line, forcing a return, to gain field position. But, overly cautious coaches will continue to kick the ball into the end zone.

Long field scoring determines the outcome of over 90 percent of all college football games. The factors above produce long field scores and are, therefore, the deterministic factors that decide the outcome of football games. Understanding these factors will help fans win debates with friends. Understanding these factors will help color commentators and TV experts make intelligent observations. Understanding these factors will help CFP committee members make good selections for the playoff.

CHAPTER SIX

Geek Numbers

What these geek numbers show—no prove—is that the traditional yardsticks of success for players and teams are fatally flawed.
—From the jacket cover of *Moneyball* **by Michael Lewis**

Now that we understand how teams score and prevent points, which is to say, how teams win football games, we can invent metrics to represent the deterministic factors to be combined in an algorithm to grade a team's performance in a specific game. The factors I invented are listed below:

1. Long Field Efficiency—the percentage of long field possessions on which a team kicks a field goal or scores a touchdown. This statistic is collected for offense and defense. On average, the 21 sample teams scored on 39.83 percent of their long field possessions while their opponents scored on 22.38 percent. Oklahoma (56.20), UCF (52.34), and Oklahoma State (51.72) led this category playing against subpar defenses while Ohio State (49.33) and Alabama (49.12) were close behind against better defenses. On the other side of the ball, Clemson surrendered scores on only 15.38 percent of its opponents' possessions. Alabama (16.15) and Wisconsin (17.04) were

next best. USC was worst in this category at 32.9 percent. Oklahoma State (32.5), Stanford (32.1) and Oklahoma (31.9) were nearly as bad.

2. Long Field Proficiency—the number of points scored on long field possessions divided by the number of long field possessions. This statistic, which rewards a team for scoring touchdowns and not settling for field goals, is a modifier for Long Field Efficiency and is collected for both offense and defense. Sample teams averaged 2.48 points per long field possession while holding their collective opponents to 1.33 points. Oklahoma (3.64), UCF (3.34), and Oklahoma State (3.18) were best against weak defenses while Alabama (3.05) and Ohio State (3.04) were quite good against better defenses and the only other teams to average

more than 3 points for every long field possession. On the defensive side of the ball, Alabama and Wisconsin gave up just 0.87 points per opponent long field possession and Clemson and Georgia were next best at 0.89 points. Stanford (1.94), Oklahoma (1.93), Oklahoma State (1.93), and USC (1.90) were easiest to score upon.

3. Explosive Plays—the number of plays covering at least twenty-five yards, including plays by the defense and special teams. The statistics is collected for offense and defense. As you might expect, UCF (73), Oklahoma State (69) and Oklahoma (67) were the most explosive teams during the 2017 season. Washington (13) and Alabama (22) surrendered the fewest explosive plays.

4. Average Field Position—the sum of all starting yard lines divided by the number of possessions, collected for offense and defense.

5. Drive stoppers. Collected only for the offense, this statistic records the percentage of long field possessions that are brought to a halt *after an initial first down*, by a turnover, a sack or a major penalty. UCF (12.5 percent) and Georgia (12.69) shot themselves in the foot least often. Wisconsin (25.95) and LSU (23.97) stopped themselves most often.

6. Third Down Avoidance Percentage. Third down plays divided by plays on first down. Measures a team's ability to achieve another first down with a first or second down play. All teams struggle on third down, but the best offenses avoid third down. Oklahoma (67.11)

and UCF (63.55) were outstanding at avoiding third downs. Michigan (47.94) and Michigan State (49.36) were least effective and the only sample teams to face third down more than half of the time.

7. Third Down Conversion Rate. Collected only for the defense, this statistic records the percentage of time that the defense "got off the field" on third down. Sample teams averaged 64.07 percent. Washington State (74.07) and Michigan (70.35) were best. Stanford (55.56) and UCF (57.98) were worst.

8. Short Field Frequency—the percentage of possessions that begin in enemy territory. Applies to both offense and defense. Alabama seemed always to be on their opponents' side of the fifty (17.99 percent of possessions), and

UCF (16.88) and Penn State (16.67) also had more than an average number of opportunities for easy scores. Stanford (3.52), LSU (3.57), and Penn State (3.85) rarely offered their opponents a fast path to points.

9. Short Field Proficiency—the number of points scored on short field possessions divided by the total number of short field possessions. Notre Dame (5.53) and Washington (5.30) shined on offense while Miami (4.90) and Penn State (4.50) yielded easiest when their backs were against wall (goal line).

10. Non-offensive Scoring—a small bonus for scoring on defense or special teams. Scoring in this category was the lowest in the eight years in which I collected the statistic. Wisconsin led the way by scoring 53 non-offensive points while Clemson, Penn State, Oklahoma,

Georgia, and Stanford surrendered no non-offensive points to their opponents.

These ten deterministic factors are sorted into offensive factors, defensive factors and factors that represent overall team play (Short Field Frequency, Non-offensive Scoring and Average Field Position). In the RPG algorithm, offense and defense are balanced and each account for 40 percent of a team's grade. Overall team play accounts for the last 20 percent of a team's grade. The best seasonal offensive grades went to Oklahoma, UCF and Oklahoma State in that order. Note again, that these teams played relatively weaker defenses. The least effective offenses (by far) belonged to Michigan State and Michigan. The best defenses belonged to Clemson, Alabama and Washington, in that order. Oklahoma, USC and Stanford had the weakest defenses, although Oklahoma State and UCF were nearly as poor. Penn State and Washington graded the best for overall team play while Washington State, Oklahoma State and Oklahoma graded the worst. From these seasonal team grades it becomes clear that the best offensive teams were also the weakest on defense and achieved their offensive numbers against relatively weak defenses. These facts will play havoc with CFP committee selections.

All Factors Are Not Equal

The 10 deterministic factors listed above— the 10 statistics that TV analysts should discuss and highlight on broadcasts and CFP committee members should use to evaluate teams—must be weighted according to their impact on the outcome of football games. The following chart depicts the relative importance of the most impactful statistics:

SAMPLE TEAMS	FIELD POSITION	DRIVE STOPPER	SHORT FIELD FREQUENCY	LONG FIELD EFFICIENCY	LONG FIELD PROFICIENCY
Won Better	89.3%	94.4%	91.4%	96.0%	97.1%
Won Worse	66.7%	53.0%	69.4%	33.9%	24.6%
Frequency	64.4%	68.2%	53.6%	76.2%	78.2%

Our learnings from this chart can be condensed into the following statements:

1. The factors that influence long field scoring—Long Field Efficiency, Long Field Proficiency, and Drive Stoppers—deserve the greatest weight in the grading algorithm. Not only did sample teams win 97.1 percent of the games in which they had better Long Field Proficiency, they lost 75.4 percent of the time when they failed to dominate that statistic. The negative impact of not dominating this statistic validates the statistic.

2. Sample teams averaged 12.18 possessions per game and started in enemy territory an average of 1.6 times per game. Therefore, sample teams had just 10.58 long field drives on which to capitalize in each game. Sustaining long field drives is so important that coaches should consider themselves in four down territory as soon as they cross the fifty yard line. As was the case for turnovers, the fear of fourth down is unwarranted. This season, sample teams and their opponents combined to convert fourth down 57.4 percent of the time, far more often than third down.

3. Although short field possessions produce easy points and keep coaches awake at night, they have less impact on winning than coaches fear. Sample teams led in this statistic barely more

than half the time and won often when their opponent had more short field chances.

4. Good field position is proven to make scoring easier but highly ranked teams overcome bad field position two times out of three. They do it by dominating long field play.

Relative Performance Grading

The calculation of offensive, defensive, and team grades for sample teams, I call Relative Performance Grading, or the RPG System for short. Each team receives a grade for each game based upon the factors that determine the outcome. This grading system can produce surprises for the experts. Much was made of the fact that LSU outgained Alabama in a 24-10 loss. Perhaps Alabama didn't deserve credit for the win, some experts said. The experts looked at the wrong numbers. Yards only matter if they produce scores. Alabama had the better long field efficiency and proficiency grades, enjoyed the only short field possession (on which it scored a touchdown), and never stopped itself on a long field drive. The RPG system gave Alabama a grade of 84.9 and LSU a grade of 66.3. In other words, neither team played particularly well but Alabama played *relatively* better and got the "W" for explainable reasons.

Game grades are summed for the season and divided by the number of games played. The grades can then be compared to rank the teams relative to one another, and thus the correct teams can be selected for and seeded in the College Football Playoff.

CHAPTER SEVEN

Football's Theory of Relativity

Everything is relative in this world …
—**Leon Trotsky**

We now know how to judge the raw playing performance of any college football team in any college football game. However, as any Philosophy 101 student will immediately ask, "Relative to what?" The answer: Relative to an opponent of unknown quality.

Fans know instinctively that not all wins are equal, and neither are all losses. Team rankings require that every playing performance grade be adjusted to reflect the strength of the opponent. The definition of a "good" team can be expanded to include this principle: *Good teams play well against opponents of known strength.*

Thus, we face the insoluble problem of strength of schedule (SOS). The committee lists SOS as one of its four primary criteria for team evaluation but also admits it has no specific metric to define any team's SOS. The committee is guessing. We hear the experts talk of "good wins" and "bad losses," or wins over the top 25, but it isn't enough to single out a game here and there. The entire body of a team's work must be evaluated. Generally, experts default to the won/lost records, but those records were discredited in Chapter Two and aren't adjusted for SOS in any event.

Wisdom of the Masses

Strictly speaking, no one knows how good any team is on opening day of football season, yet many preseason polls are published. As teams lose, they drop a few positions in the rankings, and winners backfill the available slots. Halfway through the season, an all-powerful committee begins to make its subjective guesses.

Although imperfect, the polls provide a controlled environment within which to apply our accurately composed statistical equations. However, I didn't adopt any one poll as the definitive source of SOS input. Taking the approach millennials have taught us so well, I used the wisdom of the masses to gauge the relative strength of each team.

The wisdom of the masses is embodied in the Massey College Football Ranking Composite, which homogenizes 102 ranking opinions—yes, there are that many Don Quixotes out there tilting at windmills—into a single ranked list of the 130 Football Playoff Subdivision teams. The list can be found online at http://www. masseyratings.com/cf/compare.htm. I grouped the teams into six broad categories and assigned the same SOS factor to all teams within a category. In this way, I accounted for voter error of anywhere from 10 to 15 positions within the ranking list. The categories are as follows:

1. Elite teams ranked 1-10
2. Very Good teams ranked 11-25
3. Competitive teams ranked 26-50
4. Average teams ranked 51-75
5. Below Average teams ranked 76-100
6. Weak teams ranked 101-130

A Test of Validity

Game grades for the 261 games played by the sample teams were averaged for opponents in each of the six categories. Playing performance grades were consistent for all sample teams across categories. In other words, all sample teams had lower grades against higher ranked teams and higher grades against lower ranked teams, which is a proof of the validity of this approach. A second proof is that the average grade for the sample teams increases smoothly from category to category. The one anomaly this season is that grades are lower against Category VI, the weakest teams, than against Category V, supposedly stronger teams. This has never been the case in previous seasons. Either the ranking systems misplaced stronger teams in the weakest category, or, the Category VI average was artificially deflated because USC, Iowa State and Michigan State had particularly bad games against teams in Category VI. Either way, the average grades against each category are depicted in the table below:

ELITE	VERY GOOD	COMPET-ITIVE	AVERAGE	BELOW AVERAGE	WEAK
71.98%	79.65%	86.93%	91.11%	105.92%	100.8%

Using the average grades of the six categories we can deduce that an average team was precisely 14 percent better than a below average team; that a competitive team was precisely 5 percent better than an average team; that a very good (ranked) team was precisely 10 percent better than a competitive team; and, that an elite (top 10) team was precisely 13 percent better than a very good team. The committee members do not have this precise differentiation of teams. The TV experts do not know this precise differentiation of all teams.

The Elite teams ranked in the top 10 by the composite probably belonged in the top 10 based upon the gap between that group and the Very Good teams. However, the 65 teams in Categories II, III, and IV were not that different, meaning that the TV experts' arguments that such-and-such team should be highly ranked because it played a certain number of games against the top 25 or top 50 were probably without merit. No one knows for certain that a particular team should have been in the top 25 or top 50. However, based upon the gap between Category IV and Category V, we can be fairly certain that the last 55 teams were the weakest 55 teams and were a threat to no one except one another.

The differentials between each category were used to establish the SOS adjustment factors for each category. Category V and Category VI teams were assumed to be equivalent. They were assigned an SOS value of .95 and game grades were discounted against the weakest 55 teams. The other categories were then assigned increasing values based upon their percentage of increased difficulty. The RPG system adjusts each team's playing performance grade by this factor, ensuring that great performances against weak teams are not given more credit than they deserve, and ensuring that weak performances against great teams get all the credit they deserve. This approach overcomes the fundamental weakness of the eyeball test.

Home Cooking

One final adjustment was made to the SOS factor to account for home field advantage. When playing at home, SOS factors were unadjusted, but when playing on the road, the SOS factor was incremented by 7.42 percent to account for the fact that playing performance grades were precisely 7.42 percent better on average when teams played at home. This adjustment levels the playing field and turns all games into the equivalent of home games. Neither committee members nor TV experts would have this statistic at their fingertips.

Comparative SOS

As the 2017 season came to a close and the committee's deliberations over playoff selections became serious, there was a lot of debate over which teams had played the toughest schedules. By adding and averaging the SOS values for opponents played by each team, and by incrementing the values for games played on the road, the RPG system can definitively rank the schedule strength of our 21 sample teams as follows:

1. 117.62 – Auburn
2. 117.14 – Notre Dame
3. 116.77 – Stanford
4. 115.44 – Michigan
5. 115.29 – Clemson
6. 114.83 – Ohio State
7. 114.21 – Georgia
8. 113.98 – Michigan State
9. 113.55 – Oklahoma
10. 113.52 – TCU
11. 113.50 – USC
12. 112.82 – Washington State
13. 112.80 – Miami

14. 112.45 – Penn State
15. 112.17 – Iowa State
16. 111.45 – LSU
17. 111.32 – Alabama
18. 111.18 – Wisconsin
19. 110.84 – Oklahoma State
20. 109.43 – Washington
21. 107.68 – UCF

We learn from this comparative list that all teams played a schedule equivalent to playing a top 50 team every weekend. As was so often mentioned, Alabama and Wisconsin played easier schedules than the other serious contenders for the playoff but not as much easier as TV experts would have had us believe.

CHAPTER EIGHT

Moneyball for Football

*We judge ourselves by what we feel
capable of doing, while others judge us
by what we have already done.*
—**Henry Wadsworth Longfellow**

We've identified 10 performance metrics, an SOS factor, and a road game adjustment factor and combined them into an algorithm called the Relative Performance Grading system, or RPG for short. RPG calculates a numerical grade to represent the playing performance of a team in every game whether the team wins or loses. In every game, the winning team receives a higher grade than the losing team, but the winning grade can be anywhere from 1 to 100+ and the losing grade can be anywhere from 1 to 100+ depending upon how well the teams played the game. The numerical grade distinguishes one win from another and one loss from another, just as numerical grades on school tests distinguish one passing grade from another and one failing grade from another.

Because the RPG algorithm is applied consistently and without deviation, exception or bias, to every game for every team, game grades for team A can be compared to game grades for team B. A comparison of game grades for team A and team B reveals which is the better team. A comparison of all game grades for all 130 teams in the FBS, would reveal which are the four best teams deserving of selection for the playoff.

RPG is distinguished from voting polls and human committees by its philosophy and rules. Voting polls lack consistent rules—each voter applies his or her own method to a form a subjective judgment. The CFP committee does have rules, but they are vague. It is tasked with identifying the four best teams in FBS based upon the teams' full body of work. TV experts foment conflict and confusion by suggesting alternative interpretations of this vague mission:

1. "Best" could mean best at selection time and not best over a schedule of twelve games; or,
2. "Best" could mean "most deserving", i.e. teams that win conference championships or post undefeated records.

These artificial (scripted?) arguments increase viewership which increases revenues for the networks that employ the TV experts.

The committee's mission is clear: determine which four teams played the best over an entire season of competition. However, there is no published definition of what makes team "good" or better than its competitors so the committee defaults to the eyeball test and the comparison of won/lost records. Problems with the tools the committee is given to do this job include the following:

1. Strength of Schedule. The committee admits it has no specific metric to apply. We suspect the committee counts games against teams in its own top 25 rankings and games against teams in the top 50 although we don't know which top 50 is used. This method typically ignores two-thirds to

three-quarters of each team's schedule which is assumed to be equivalent to all other teams except in those cases when the committee somehow suspects that Alabama and Wisconsin have played weak overall schedules.

2. Head-to-head results. Although head-to-head results receive a permanent entry in the record books, and although bragging rights persist for years, there is nothing definitive or permanent about an individual victory. A win does not mean that the winning team is forever better than the losing team. It means that the winning team played relatively better than the losing team on game day under a specific set of circumstances. Oklahoma's win over Ohio State in Columbus on the second Saturday of the 2017 season, punctuated by Baker Mayfield's plant of the Sooner flag in

the Buckeyes' logo, seared an indelible image on the minds of the committee members. In their minds, Oklahoma became the better team forever. RPG did not watch that game on TV. RPG graded the performances of the two teams—110.84 for Oklahoma and 74.79 for Ohio State—and combined those grades with all others for each team to determine which was the better team (based upon a "full body of work"). RPG is not burdened with inbred thinking.

3. Results against common opponents. This would be a good point of comparison if the committee had a tool for comparing results. The committee has no such tool, so it defaults to the fallible eyeball test and the discredited won/lost record. RPG can compare game grades for two teams against

common opponents. Had RPG been used by the committee following the 2016 season, it would have shown that Michigan had better results than Ohio State against common opponents. That's right, Michigan, not Penn State. Swayed by Penn State's Big Ten conference championship, the committee compared the wrong two teams for the final spot in the 2016 playoffs when it compared Ohio State to Penn State. It should have compared Michigan to Ohio State, both of which had better resumes than the conference champion. Using the RPG system as its guide, the committee would have chosen Michigan. Of course, the committee couldn't bring itself to do that because Ohio State had defeated Michigan in the last regular season game and that brings us full circle to the fallacy of head-to-head results.

4. Conference championships. The Power Five conferences, except for the Big 12, have expanded to the point at which they can't play round-robin schedules. The conferences are divided into divisions and no clear regular season champion can be identified using won/lost records. Turning lemons into lemonade, the conferences, now including the Big 12, established conference championship games which increased revenues. The committee—and the fans, and the TV experts—assigns illogical importance to the championship games as though the game has more meaning than all others. Of course, RPG knows before the championship games are played, which team in each conference has had

the best season based upon a full body of work. Nonetheless, RPG gives each winner of these games a 10 percent boost in its playing performance grade, not because the game has special significance, but because reaching the game proves the value of a team's full body of work. Then the system combines the grade with all other grades because the championship game is just another game in a team's full body of work.

If the precept of a full body of work were to be applied rigorously and consistently, every game played would matter and would matter equally. Unfortunately, the human brain doesn't function that way. Inevitably, humans suffer from recency bias, i.e. what have you done lately. The term was coined to describe stock market investor behavior influenced more by recent results than by historical results. This holds true in college football as well. Inevitably, a team's results in its November games has more influence on our evaluation than do the games it played in September. Losing early in the season is okay; losing late will be punished; winning late will be rewarded. TV experts defend this bias by claiming that some teams improve over the course of a season and the committee should take the four best teams on selection Sunday and not the four teams with the best full body of work.

The committee could, indeed, adopt this approach but it would be skating on thin ice. For every Auburn whose quarterback play improved over the course of the season, there is an Ohio State whose chart of playing performance week after week looks like a topical graph of the Rocky Mountains. In an experiment, I modified the RPG system to decrease credit for each team's first four games and increase credit for its last four games. The surprising result was that the modification had no impact on the seasonal rankings of our 21 sample teams. There was no change because there are far more Clemsons—boringly consistent—and Ohio States—up and down like a roller coaster—than there are Auburns with a hockey stick trajectory.

The CFP committee—a motley crew comprised of ex-coaches (5), current and former athletics directors (5), a former reporter, a former NCAA executive, and a university president—is tasked with performing an impossible mission given its lack of suitable tools and detailed, definitive rules. This year the full committee was unable to discharge its duties. Three members recused themselves because of ties to schools under consideration. That left ten members to make a momentous decision as surprising as opening Forrest Gump's box of chocolates. If the committee had used the RPG system to determine the four best teams, a committee vote would have been unnecessary because the committee would have had definitive proof to support the selections.

For consistency and fairness, the RPG System adheres to a short list of simple rules:

1. Full Body of Work
    Every Saturday counts. Every game is graded, and every game carries the same weight except for conference championship games which carry slightly more weight but are averaged with all other games.

2. Flat-footed Start
    All teams begin the season without a grade and then earn grades for performance in real games. Preseason poll positions do not provide teams with advantages before they accomplish anything. The CFP committee seems to agree with this principle as they publish

their first rankings after the games of week ten, after a partial body of work is available for evaluation. RPG publishes rankings after week one but based upon actual performance. As a result, the early rankings can confuse fans and poll voters alike. For example, Notre Dame was ranked No. 4 and TCU was ranked No. 5 after week one although neither had been included in the AP preseason rankings. The two teams had simply played well in their first games and the RPG rankings reflected that fact. On the other hand, teams that get off to a slow start, as Georgia did, must play their way to the top. Which Georgia did.

3. Head-to-Head Results Have No Intrinsic Importance

Fans are sometimes confused when their favorite team is ranked behind a rival it defeated but head-to-head results create knotty problems. Notre Dame thrashed USC, which defeated Stanford twice, which defeated Notre Dame handily. In what sequence would those teams be ranked based upon head-to-head results?

4. Late Season Games Are Not More Important than Early Season Games

   A football season is small sample of games, so all games must be treated equally. Unfortunately, human perception is swayed by recency bias, but the RPG system is not.

5. SOS Is Continuously Updated

   If team grades are to be based upon a full body of work, SOS must also be based upon the full body of work of opponents. Alabama did not get credit for defeating a Florida State team incorrectly thought to be a top

10 team at the start of the season. Alabama received credit for defeating a team that proved itself to be top 50 (Category III).

6. RPG Grades Replace Wins and Losses
   When a team outplays its opponent (and wins the game), it receives a higher grade than its opponent. When a team is outplayed by its opponent (and loses the game), it receives a lower grade than its opponent. In all games, both teams are graded for performance and neither team receives a misleading "W" or "L" to conceal the quality of its play. RPG can, of course, add up the number of times that a team had a higher game grade than its opponent and put that number in the "W" column. It can also add up the number of times a team received a lower game grade and put that number in the "L"

column. The statistic would not be useful for comparison purposes.

CHAPTER NINE

Cinderella's Ball

Turn and peep, turn and peep,
There's blood within the shoe,
The shoe it is too small for her,
The true bride waits for you.
—From *Cinderella* by Jacob and
Wilhelm Grimm

The First Reveal

After judiciously watching ten weeks of play on the field, eight games for most teams, the CFP committee revealed its first rankings of the 2017 season. Fans generally accepted the rankings as a noncontroversial start to the race for playoff positions. The RPG system, however, disagreed sharply with the committee's ranking sequence. According to RPG, the committee had made several classic evaluation mistakes, noted in the table below.

TEAM	CFP RANK	ERROR	RPG RANK
Georgia	1	Head-to-head	4
Alabama	2	Brand bias	1
Notre Dame	3	Eyeball test	5
Clemson	4		10
Oklahoma	5		15
Ohio State	6		3
Penn State	7		6
TCU	8		11
Wisconsin	9	Record Bias	14
Miami	10	Record Bias	13

Notre Dame's claim to fame was a thrashing of grossly overrated USC (a big brand team) and Georgia's climb to the top was propelled by a one-point victory in South Bend over the Irish. Later the Irish would fade to mediocrity and the Georgia win would carry less weight.

Clemson established a pattern of building a first half lead and then fading in the second halves of its games. Its ugly win over Auburn was an excuse to rank them at No. 4 despite an ugly loss to Syracuse, a team that would not win another game all season. As the reigning national champion, Clemson enjoyed an outsized helping of brand recognition not justified by consistently mediocre playing performance grades.

Dazzled by the zeros in the loss columns for Wisconsin and Miami, the committee allowed those two teams to float into the top ten like overstuffed helium balloons. In fact, Wisconsin had played down to the weakest schedule among ranked teams and Miami's playing performances were the very definition of winning ugly. Both mistakes would return to haunt the committee.

The most egregious ranking error committed that first week of rankings was the positioning of Oklahoma in the No. 5 spot. Oklahoma's week three/game two victory over Ohio State must have been the excuse for the Sooners' ranking at No.5 because the rest of their resume was decidedly unimpressive. After the win in Columbus, Oklahoma surrendered 41 points to Baylor, one of the weakest 30 teams in FBS, lost to an Iowa State team that would finish 7-5, and squeaked past mediocre Texas and Kansas State before beating weak Texas Tech. By that point Oklahoma's defense had sunk to dead last among sample teams but their offense pleased the committee's eyeballs and earned the Sooners the largest margin of ranking error.

Compounded Ranking Errors and a Possible Conspiracy

Over the next three weeks, Oklahoma beat in-state rival Oklahoma State on the road, overrated TCU, and Kansas, another of the worst 30 teams in FBS. In the CFP rankings, Oklahoma rose to No. 4 while RPG promoted the Sooners to No. 12. How much credit should a team get for giving up 52 points to Oklahoma State?

In weeks eleven and twelve Clemson advanced somewhat in the RPG rankings from No. 10 to No. 8 with successive, albeit pedestrian, wins over top 50 teams. The CFP committee promoted Clemson all the way to No. 2. At the same time, ACC rival Miami rose to No. 3 in the committee rankings after victories over two ranked teams. In the RPG rankings, Miami only made it to No. 10 because they had not played well in the two wins.

In the committee rankings, Clemson and Miami were now poised for a winner-take-all confrontation in the ACC title game. Wisconsin had improbably risen to No. 5 in the committee rankings because they still had not lost a game. They still hadn't played any tough opponents either. Wisconsin was No. 13 in the RPG rankings. The other Big Ten contender, Ohio State, had dropped from No. 6 to No. 13 in the committee rankings after a devastating loss at Iowa. The Buckeyes only fell from No. 3 to No. 6 in the RPG rankings because they had a reservoir of great game grades to balance the loss.

Alabama had assumed the No. 1 spot in both committee rankings and RPG rankings at this point as Georgia had been crushed by Auburn and had fallen to No. 7. On the strength of that win, Auburn rose to No. 6 in the committee rankings, giving the SEC three teams in the top seven with two weeks left in the regular season.

That was too much for people tired of SEC domination. In week thirteen, Clemson blew out The Citadel while Miami struggled to a come-from-behind win over Virginia. Inexplicably, Miami was promoted to No.2 and Clemson was demoted to No. 3. Immediately, conspiracy theorists interpreted the move as a way to block Alabama or keep two SEC teams from making the playoffs. The thinking was that two SEC teams could survive remaining games between Alabama and Auburn and the winner of that game versus Georgia. If Alabama beat Auburn but lost to Georgia, both division winners could reach the playoff. But, a close win by Clemson over previously unbeaten Miami could justify ranking two ACC teams ahead of Alabama.

The other inexplicable committee move was the position swap between Oklahoma (No.

4 to No. 5) and Wisconsin (No. 5 to No. 4). The move was either unjustified homage to Wisconsin's unbeaten record or a tip of the cap to the Big Ten which was in danger of being locked out of the playoffs.

The Best Laid Plans of Mice and Men

The committee's mystifying machinations came to naught in week fourteen as Miami stumbled at lowly-regarded Pitt and Alabama choked in Jordan-Hare Stadium. In week ten, the committee had guessed that Georgia was the best team in the country and then Auburn demolished them. In week twelve, the committee guessed that Alabama was the best team in the country and then Auburn demolished them. So, the Tigers should be No. 1, right? Yep, the other Tigers. Once upon a time in a land far, far away, Clemson had limped to a win over an Auburn team with a rookie quarterback that didn't yet know what War Eagle meant. The committee couldn't forget that and ranked Clemson No. 1 and Auburn No. 2. The comparative rankings after fourteen weeks of play are below:

TEAM	CFP RANK	ERROR	RPG RANK
Clemson	1	Head-to-head	7
Auburn	2	Head-to-head	6
Oklahoma	3	Eyeball test	10
Wisconsin	4	Record bias	9
Alabama	5	Head-to-head	1
Georgia	6		8
Miami	7	Record Bias	15
Ohio State	8	Bad loss	2
Penn State	9	Inexplicable	4
USC	10	Brand bias	18

The committee's heavy-handed manipulations created an artificial situation in which the conference championship games appeared to be playoff quarterfinals. An Oklahoma loss to TCU in the Big 12 title game would throw a wrench in the works but the ACC, SEC and

Big Ten winners would join Oklahoma if the Sooners won. The TV experts were sure of it.

Once again, the games did not play out as expected. Oklahoma claimed a spot in the playoff with an easy win over TCU. Clemson destroyed Miami and any hopes the Hurricanes could become a second ACC entrant in the playoff. Although Georgia had been decimated by Auburn only two weeks earlier, the Bulldogs now smashed the Tigers convincingly. Three teams were probably in.

As expected, despite being ranked lower, Ohio State defeated Wisconsin for the Big Ten title. To their credit, the Badgers put up a good fight and had two chances to steal a late victory. Nonetheless, most fans went to bed that Saturday night convinced by TV experts that Ohio State had won a play-in game. The committee members weren't as sure. At 2:30 a.m. Central Time in Grapevine, Texas, the men retired after hours of exhausting deliberation.

They had reached a tentative decision they would confirm in the morning.

In the early afternoon hours on selection Sunday, ESPN delivered the shocking announcement: Alabama was in and Ohio State was out. The committee overlooked Bama's loss on the road to Auburn but couldn't stomach Ohio State's dismemberment in Iowa City. When comparing just those two games, the committee correctly surmised that Alabama performed better than did Ohio State, 65.4 to 57.51. However, in comparing their seasons, the committee got it wrong. Going into championship weekend Alabama led Ohio State by a slim margin. Alabama then spent its weekend recruiting five star athletes while Ohio State defeated No. 4 Wisconsin. In the RPG rankings, Ohio State slipped past the Tide. When comparing the two teams on a full body of work basis, the committee got it wrong.

But wait! There's more to the story. The committee compared the wrong two teams. As you can see from the chart above, Alabama and Ohio State were comfortably in the playoff before conference championship games were played. Georgia leapfrogged Alabama with its beat down of Auburn and reserved its position in the playoff. That should have left the committee to compare ACC champ Clemson to Big 12 champ Oklahoma. Based upon their own rankings, the committee would correctly have chosen Clemson, but the committee would have hated leaving the exciting Sooner offense out of the mix. The Sooners were ranked No. 10 by RPG before the conference championship game and No. 8 after their win over TCU. At No. 4, after its win over Miami, Clemson would have been the easy choice, allowing committee members to get a full night's rest and enjoy a stress-free Sunday brunch. The chart below reveals the full, final rankings for all 21 sample teams.

TEAM	RPG RANK	RPG GRADE	CFP RANK	ERROR
Ohio State	1	107.00	5	Bad loss
Georgia	2	106.80	3	
Alabama	3	106.42	4	
Clemson	4	105.32	1	Brand bias
Washington	5	104.84	12	Unknown
Penn State	6	104.15	9	Unknown
UCF	7	104.14	10	Conf. bias
Oklahoma	8	102.46	2	Eyeball test
Auburn	9	100.38	7	
Wisconsin	10	98.77	7	Record bias
Oklahoma St	11	98.51	17	
Notre Dame	12	97.82	14	
Stanford	13	96.29	15	
TCU	14	94.15	13	
Miami	15	92.61	11	Record bias
LSU	16	91.81	16	
USC	17	90.06	8	Brand bias
Iowa St	18	89.45	NR	
Washington St	19	88.70	21	
Michigan	20	86.09	NR	
Michigan St	21	85.95	18	

NR = Not Ranked

The CFP rankings require Georgia to travel cross-country to meet Oklahoma in the unfamiliar surroundings of the Rose Bowl while Alabama and Clemson play familiar foes in the friendly confines of Alabama's home-away-from-home, the Sugar Bowl in New Orleans. Had the RPG rankings prevailed, Ohio State would have hosted Clemson in its traditional destination, the Rose Bowl, while Alabama and Georgia would have played the SEC title-game-that-didn't-happen in their traditional destination, the Sugar Bowl.

After hours of misguided deliberation, the CFP committee had selected Alabama instead of Ohio State. The next day, the ESPN Football Power Index (FPI), set the playoff probability to win the championship at:

1. Alabama – 35 percent

2. Georgia – 24 percent
3. Clemson – 23 percent
4. Oklahoma – 18 percent

In other words, the FPI agreed with the RPG relative rankings of the four teams and second-guessed the committee's unnecessary head-scratching over Alabama.

The committee's rankings changed the course of history. Since Ohio State wasn't in, it couldn't win what it may have deserved to win. As fate would have it, the two best teams in the playoff gave fans the title game they deserved.

The Forgotten Teams

The committee's selection of Oklahoma can be explained by the unreliable eyeball test and an unconscious bias toward offensive production. The committee's low regard for Washington and Penn State is harder to understand. Penn State's two losses were to ranked teams on the road by a total of four points. Washington also lost twice, to a ranked Stanford team and a temporarily ranked Arizona State team. Both games were competitive. The RPG system liked both teams very much and they should be congratulated for seasons that nearly deserved playoff participation.

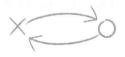

CHAPTER TEN

Cinderella's Slipper

*When somebody says, 'This is not about
money, it's the principle of the thing,'
it's about money.*
—Kin Hubbard

To its credit, the oft-maligned BCS crowned seven champions that were ranked No. 2 entering the title game. Those teams would have been denied titles in favor of undeserving teams ranked No. 1 in the poll voting era, meaning the polls may have been wrong nearly half the time. If we extrapolate, 11 of the poll era's 25 champions may have been wrongly coronated.

Moving from a two-team playoff to a four-team playoff moves the boundary of mistaken selection from the No. 2/No. 3 positions to the No. 4/No. 5 positions. The move does not eliminate fan criticism. The CFP committee was criticized for including Florida State in 2014. The CFP committee was criticized for manipulating the standings at the 11th hour and excluding TCU from the 2015 playoff. The CFP committee was criticized for including Ohio State in the 2016 playoff. The committee should have been criticized for excluding Ohio State from the 2017 playoff. The committee suffers from a lack of tools and rules and is handcuffed by inside-the-box thinking. It cannot be expected to make perfect decisions.

The four-team playoff system is a welcome gift to fans, but it is also a well-designed mechanism to protect the financial interests of bowl organizers, conferences, and television networks. No changes to this system will occur if those financial interests are threatened.

Inevitably, television networks will find a way—money—to convince bowl organizers and conferences to expand to an eight-team playoff structure. Arguments against the expanded format simply don't pass the smell test. The FCS subdivision of the NCAA conducts a 24-team playoff and hands out a trophy with the NCAA's initials on it. Each year a team wins at least four playoff games to capture the title. If an FCS team can do it, Alabama, Ohio State, and USC can too.

Dan Wetzel of Yahoo Sports suggested that the easiest way to fit an eight-team playoff into existing schedules is to eliminate conference championship games and replace them with the playoff quarterfinals in early December. My suggestion is to rotate the four quarterfinal games through the five power conference championship venues to minimize loss of revenues. The semi-finals and finals would progress as currently conducted.

The ultimate test—Cinderella's Slipper—should consist of an accurate ranking system—like the RPG—selecting the eight best teams in the land irrespective of conference or bowl affiliation. This won't happen. The five power conference champions will automatically qualify and the best team from the Group of Five conferences will be nominated by a committee. This approach will satisfy most fans but will not solve other problems. The CFP committee will be left to select two at-large teams, basically the same task that the BCS failed at. The committee's selections will always cause controversy. The committee will also be left to seed the teams in brackets. As the size of the field increases, seeding becomes a determining factor in the outcome.

How should the conference champions and at-large teams be selected for the playoff? By a faultless and impartial performance ranking method like the RPG system, of course. Throughout the fall the RPG weekly rankings and my blog posts can be found at www.nemosnumbers.com.

It's entirely possible that fans do not want a factual, definitive ranking system that eliminates all controversy. It's entirely possible that the heated arguments among fans, TV experts, and committee members are an essential component of the college football experience and would be missed if indisputable facts replaced them. In that case, I humbly offer the RPG system as a factual counterpoint to subjective opinion.

~ The End ~

ABOUT THE AUTHOR

Mike Nemeth is a retired Information Technology executive living in the Atlanta suburbs with his wife, Angie, and their rescue dog, Sophie. His previous works  include the Amazon bestselling crime thriller *Defiled*, its sequel *The Undiscovered Country*, and the groundbreaking book about the NCAA Men's Basketball Tournament, *128 Billion to 1*.

Morgan James
Speakers Group

↗ www.TheMorganJamesSpeakersGroup.com

We connect Morgan James published
authors with live and online events
and audiences who will benefit
from their expertise.

Morgan James makes all of our titles
available through the Library for All
Charity Organization.

www.LibraryForAll.org

Printed in the USA
CPSIA information can be obtained
at www.ICGtesting.com
JSHW082357140824
68134JS00020B/2136

9 781683 508571